EMBRACING AN
ALTERNATIVE
ORTHODOXY

Richard Rohr
on the Legacy of St. Francis

A 5-Session Study by Richard Rohr with Tim Scorer

Morehouse Education Resources,
a division of Church Publishing Incorporated
Editorial Offices: 600 Grant Street, Suite 630, Denver, CO 80203

For catalogs and orders call:
1-800-672-1789
www.MorehouseEducation.org

Litany on page 77 from *Psalms for Praying: An Invitation to Wholeness* © 1996 by Nan C. Merrill (Harrisburg, PA: Continuum, an imprint of Bloomsbury Publishing Inc.) Used by permission.

Photos on pages 9, 10, 30, 46, 60 and 74 © 2014 by Dirk deVries. All rights reserved. Used by permission.

ISBN-13: 978-1-60674-140-5

TABLE OF CONTENTS

QUICK GUIDE TO THE HANDBOOK

TEN things to know as you begin to work with this resource:

1. HANDBOOK + WORKBOOK

This handbook is a guide to the group process as well as a workbook for everyone in the group.

2. A FIVE-SESSION RESOURCE

Each of the five sessions presents a distinct topic for focused group study and conversation.

3. DVD-BASED RESOURCE

The teaching content in each session comes in the form of input by Fr. Richard Rohr and response by members of a small group on a DVD recording of just over 30 minutes in length.

4. EVERYONE GETS EVERYTHING

This handbook addresses everyone in the group, not one group leader. There is no separate "Leader's Guide."

5. GROUP FACILITATION

The creators of this resource assume that someone will be designated as group facilitator for each session. You may choose the same person or a different person for each of the five sessions.

6. TIME FLEXIBILITY

Each of the five sessions is flexible and can be between one hour and two or more hours in length: however, if you intend to cover all the material presented, you will need the full two hours.

7. BUILD YOUR OWN SESSION

Prior to the session it is advisable for one or more members of the group to determine what to include in the group meeting time. In some cases the session outline presents options from which you can choose. In other cases the material is organized as a progression through the three or four main topics presented by Richard Rohr.

8. WITHIN EACH TOPIC IN A SESSION

Each segment in a session features a mix of input from Richard Rohr and the other members of the small group in the video, plus questions for discussion or other creative activities to guide individual and group reflection.

9. BEFORE THE SESSION

Each session opens with five activities for participants to use as personal preparation prior to the session.

10. CLOSING AND BEYOND

Each session ends with an option that is a suggestion for ongoing personal engagement with the topic of the session. A closing prayer is provided. Groups are encouraged to follow a prayer practice that reflects their own traditions and experience.

BEYOND THE "QUICK GUIDE"

Helpful information and guidance for anyone using this resource:

1. HANDBOOK + WORKBOOK

This handbook is a guide to the group process as well as a workbook for everyone in the group.

• We hope the handbook gives you all the information you need to feel confident in shaping the program to work for you and your fellow group members.

• The work space provided in the handbook encourages you...
— to respond to leading questions.
— to write or draw your own reflections.
— to note the helpful responses of other group members.

2. FIVE-SESSION RESOURCE

This resource presents Richard Rohr's insights on Alternative Orthodoxy, framed as five distinct topics of study:

1. Atonement Theology
2. Eco-Spirituality
3. The Cosmic Christ
4. Orthodoxy vs. Orthopraxy
5. Mysticism over Moralism

3. DVD-BASED RESOURCE

The teaching content in each session comes in the form of input by Richard Rohr and response by members of a small group. The video for each runs just over 30 minutes in length.

Richard Rohr's focused and engaging presentations stimulate thoughtful and heartfelt conversation among his listeners.

The edited conversations present group sharing that builds on Richard's initial teaching. They are intended to present to you a model of small group interaction that is personal, respectful and engaged.

• You will notice that the participants in the DVD group also become our teachers. In many cases, quotes from the group members enrich the teaching component of this resource. This will also happen in your group—you will become teachers for one another.

• We hope that the DVD presentations spark conversations about those things that matter most to those who are striving to understand matters of faith in the 21st century.

4. EVERYONE GETS EVERYTHING

The handbook addresses everyone in the group, not one group leader. There is no separate "Leader's Guide."

Unlike many small group resources, this one makes no distinction between material for the group facilitator and for the participants. Everyone has it all! We believe this empowers you and your fellow group members to share creatively in the leadership.

5. GROUP FACILITATION

We designed this for you to designate a group facilitator for each session. It does not have to be the same person for all five sessions, because everyone has all the material. It is, however, essential that you and the other group members are clear about who is facilitating each session. One or two people still have to be responsible for these kinds of things:

- making arrangements for the meeting space (see notes on Meeting Space, p. 12)
- setting up the space to be conducive to conversations in a diverse small group community
- creating and leading an opening to the session (see notes on Opening, p. 12)
- helping the group decide on which elements of the guide to focus on in that session
- facilitating the group conversation for that session
- keeping track of the time
- calling the group members to attend to the standards established for the group life (see notes on Group Standards, p. 12)
- creating space in the conversation for all to participate

- keeping the conversation moving along so that the group covers all that it set out to do
- ensuring that time is taken for a satisfying closing to the session
- making sure that everyone is clear about date, location and focus for the next session
- following up with people who missed the session

6. TIME FLEXIBILITY

Each of the five sessions is flexible and can be between one hour and two or more hours in length: however, if you intend to cover all the material presented, you will need the full two hours.

We designed this resource for your group to tailor it to fit the space available in the life of the congregation or community using it. That might be Sunday morning for an hour before or after worship, two hours on a weekday evening, or 90 minutes on a weekday morning.

Some groups might decide to spend two sessions on one of the five major topics. There's enough material in each of the five outlines to do that. Rushing to get through more than the time comfortably allows results in people not having the opportunity to speak about the things that matter to them.

7. BUILD YOUR OWN SESSION

Prior to the session it is advisable for one or more members of the group to determine what to include in the group meeting time. The session outline presents options from which you can choose.

- One or two people might take on the responsibility of shaping the session based on what they think will appeal to the group members. This responsibility could be shared from week to week.
- The group might take time at the end of one session to look ahead and decide on what they will cover in the next session. In the interest of time, it might be best to assign this planning to a couple members of the group.
- You might decide to do your personal preparation for the session (the five activities in "Before the Session"), and when everyone comes together for the session, proceed on the basis of what topics interested people the most.

8. WITHIN EACH TOPIC IN A SESSION

Each segment in a session features a mix of input from Richard Rohr and the other members of the small group in the video, plus questions for discussion or other creative activities to guide individual and group reflection.

You will recognize that the activities and topics in the study guide emerge both from the structured teaching of Fr. Rohr as well as the informal and spontaneous conversation of the group members. This parallels the process of your group, which will be initially led by the content of the DVD and the study guide, but then branch off in directions that emerge spontaneously from the particular life of your group.

9. BEFORE THE SESSION

Each session opens with five activities for participants to use as personal preparation prior to the session.

- We intend these activities to open in you some aspect of the topic being considered in the upcoming session. This may lead you to feel more confident when addressing the issue in the group.
- Sometimes these questions are the same as ones raised in the context of the session. They offer the opportunity for you to do some personal reflection both before and/or after engaging in the group conversation on that topic.

10. CLOSING AND BEYOND

Each session has a final reflective option for participants to take from the session and use as an extension of their learning. These offer a disciplined way for each participant to continue to harvest the riches of the group conversation.

A closing prayer is provided at the end of each session. Groups are encouraged to follow a prayer practice that reflects their own traditions and experience.

Another aspect of closing is *evaluation*. This is not included in an intentional way in the design of the sessions; however, evaluation is such a natural and satisfying thing to do that it could be included as part of the discipline of closing each session. It's as simple as taking time to respond to these questions:

- What insights am I taking from this session?
- What contributed to my learning?
- What will I do differently as a result of my being here today?

POINTERS ON FACILITATION

1. Meeting Space

- Take time to prepare the space for the group. When people come into a space that has been prepared for them, they trust the hospitality, resulting in a willingness to bring the fullness of themselves into the conversation. Something as simple as playing recorded music as people arrive will contribute to this sense of "a space prepared for you."
- Think about how the space will encourage a spirit of reverence, intimacy and care. Will there be a table in the center of the circle where a candle can be lit each time the group meets? Is there room for other symbols that emerge from the group's life?

2. Opening

- In the opening session, take time to go around the circle and introduce yourselves in some way.
- Every time a group comes together again, it takes each member time to feel fully included. Some take longer than others. An important function of facilitation is to help this happen with ease, so people find themselves participating fully in the conversation as soon as possible. We designed these sessions with this in mind. Encouraging people to share in the activity proposed under *Group Life* is one way of supporting that feeling of inclusion.
- The ritual of opening might include the lighting of a candle, an opening prayer, the singing of a hymn where appropriate, and the naming of each person present.

3. Group Standards

- There are basic standards in group life that are helpful to name when a new group begins. Once they are named, you can always come back to them as a point of reference if necessary. Here are two basics:
  — Everything that is said in this group remains in the group. *(confidentiality)*
  — We will begin and end at the time agreed. *(punctuality)*
- Are there any others that you need to name as you begin? Sometimes standards emerge from the life of the group and need to be named when they become evident, otherwise they are just assumed.

The people who know God well—mystics, hermits, prayerful people, those who risk everything to find God—always meet a lover, not a dictator.

—Richard Rohr,
Everything Belongs: The Gift of Contemplative Prayer

SESSION | 1

ATONEMENT THEOLOGY

BEFORE THE SESSION

Many participants like to come to the group conversation after considering individually some of the issues that will be raised. The following five reflective activities are intended to open your mind, memories and emotions regarding some aspects of this session's topic. Use the space provided here to note your reflections.

1. Traditional atonement theology can be summed up by the roadside sign that announces "Jesus died for our sins." This theology requires that there be a transaction—a deal—so that God can love what God created. God's acceptance is purchased through the death of Jesus. Where have you encountered this theology? What place does it have in your belief system and in your faith community?

2. An alternative view of atonement *(at-one-ment)* tells us that God's love has always come without conditions and still does. No deal is necessary. As you go through these days, engaged in the ordinary tasks of living, watch for signs of the overwhelming, unconditional love that God has for the creation, for you and for all that you choose to love.

3. Jesus models for us a life path that is all about letting go of illusion and pretense (the small false self) and embracing the fullness of life—including death—in a way that the true self has space to emerge and to be known ever more fully. How is your "self" doing as you follow this Christ path from the false to the true?

4. *Quid Pro Quo* names a way of dealing with things "tit for tat"—an eye for an eye. Retributive justice is like that, ensuring that the wrongdoer be adequately punished according to the laws of the state. Restorative justice, on the other hand, focuses on the just restoration of relationship in which the concerns of all those affected by the wrong done are addressed. Restorative justice makes space for the exercise of grace. Where have you seen grace being given space to make a difference recently?

5. Richard Rohr is a Franciscan friar, hence the subtitle of this series: "On the Legacy of St. Francis." What can you find out through the Internet about the following: *Rohr, Franciscans, St. Francis.*

The theme of this study is "Embracing An Alternative Orthodoxy." You have come together as a group, ready to uncover some responses to this question: What are the dynamics of alternative orthodoxy in the second decade of the 21st century?

If this is a new group meeting for the first time, take a few minutes to introduce yourselves in two ways:
• by telling your name
• by telling one thing that attracted you to participate in this program

In September of 2013, another group met in Albuquerque, New Mexico, to learn with Richard Rohr and to grapple with the same issues that are on your agenda for these five sessions.

Moving from left to right as you will see them on the screen, they are Tim Scorer (moderator and author of this study guide), Doug Travis, Jennifer Murphy-Dye, Joe Alarid, Suzanne Gutierrez, Raymond Raney and Fr. Richard Rohr. You won't hear from each person in every session, but over the course of five sessions you will hear contributions from all six participants in the group.

Before selecting from the following options, *watch the entire portion of the DVD for Session 1.*

OPTION 1: COMING TO TERMS WITH ATONEMENT

Historical Background to Two Approaches to Atonement

Franciscans had an alternative understanding of the atonement from their inception 800 years ago. The Roman Church did not deem this heretical. In the broad-mindedness of the 13th Century, it was possible to have a minority position as well as a majority one without anyone being kicked out of the Church.

Mainline Protestantism by and large fully accepted the majority position on atonement. Because Franciscans were something of a sideshow within Catholicism, they were never as invested in it as most evangelical Christians are today.

1. Richard Rohr on the Majority Position on Atonement

Some insights that Richard offers in his introduction:
- The mainline position on atonement that anyone in any denomination has probably been influenced by is summed up in the phrase you see on highway signs: "Jesus died for our sins."
- Traditional atonement theology claims that there needed to be a transaction for God to love what God created. God's love had to be purchased in some way.
- This theology is based on many quotes from the New Testament where this kind of language is being used: *ransom, satisfaction, paying the price* and *died for us.*

- In the first 1,000 years of Christianity, the normal Christian consensus was that the debt was being paid *to the devil.*
- It was Anselm of Canterbury (1033–1109) who, in his paper *Cur Deus Homo (Why Did God Become Human),* made a case for the debt being paid *to God*, not the devil.
- Atonement made sense to Jewish people from their experience of Temple sacrifice, where there was some transaction necessary because the language and metaphors were already part of their tradition.

2. The Franciscan Minority Position on Atonement Theology

Having offered an introduction to traditional atonement theology, Richard then proceeds to offer a critique of it by presenting the Franciscan view of atonement beginning with a quote from Franciscan John Duns Scotus, one of the most important philosopher-theologians of the High Middle Ages:

> Jesus did not come to change the mind of God about humanity, but to change the mind of humanity about God.

Here are seven quotes from Richard's presentation of the minority Franciscan position on atonement:

1: God organically loved what God created from the first moment of the Big Bang. There was an inherent love relationship between God and creation. God wanted to show God's Self in material creation.

2: The Christ existed from all eternity. The Christ was the first idea in the mind of God.

3: Jesus is the image of the invisible God from all eternity. There is simply a union to be named: *at-one-ment*.

4: The first idea in the mind of God is to reveal who God is. Jesus is the revelation of God's Plan A. Jesus is not a mop-up exercise after Adam and Eve ate that darn apple!

5: When we say in traditional atonement theology that there needs to be a transaction for God to love what God created, we create a barrier to mystical thinking and to the understanding of the unconditional love of God.

6: The traditional atonement theory doesn't say much good about God. It suggests that God doesn't have an inherent love for what God created; God is "pissed off," so to speak.

7: No transaction was necessary. No blood sacrifice was necessary. No atonement is necessary. There is no bill to be paid.

1. Richard states:

> When you make these challenges to traditional atonement theology people feel like you're taking away their faith because many people have based their understanding of Jesus on this.

This may be true for you too. Perhaps this challenge to traditional atonement theology comes as a shock. It may take a while to fully absorb Richard's challenge and to consider the implications for your own theology. What impact does Richard's critique of atonement theology have on you?

2. Now that we have these two conflicting approaches to atonement laid out so clearly, what do you affirm for yourself about these matters:
   - God and creation
   - Christ in creation
   - Jesus as revelation
   - the death of Jesus
   - atonement vs. at-one-ment

3. Richard says:

> *When we say in atonement theology that*
> *there needs to be a transaction for God to*
> *love what God created, we create a barrier to*
> *mystical thinking and to the understanding*
> *of the unconditional love of God.*

In other words, there can be no conditions
on God's love. That love existed from the
beginning for all creation, and it is still here
for you billions of years later. It did not need
to be bought, and it will never need to be
bought. What convinces you of the love of
God, fully present with no conditions?

OPTION 2: THE SELF-EMPTYING WAY

Doug asks:

> *Jesus asks that the cup be passed and then goes on to say, "nevertheless, not my will but your will." So he willingly dies. There is implicit in that a notion that, in some measure, God required of Jesus that he die. How does that fit in to plan A?*

Richard responds:

> *I wouldn't say that God required it. I would say that* reality requires the letting go of what I call the "false self." *Reality requires the letting go of illusion and pretense. In my Christology I would say that Jesus died willingly, surrendering the Jesus "small self" so the Christ "universal self" could be born. In doing that* he models for all of us the same path. *I know this isn't attractive to Western Christians,* but death is part of the deal. *That's not a negative statement, a morbid, punishing or threatening statement. It's just that animals know it, trees know it—the cycles of death and life. What we see in Jesus is a willing surrendering to that, an embracing of that.*

Raymond adds:

> *Paul talks about Jesus emptying himself—in Greek,* kenosis. *The actual atonement that Jesus did was the emptying of himself to do what God wanted.*

Richard responds:

> *You name it that way, and suddenly Buddhists take notice. We're saying the same thing and, of course, if truth is one (as it has to be or it's not truth), wouldn't that make sense that the great religions are coming to very similar conclusions. So using that word "emptying" from Philippians is right on if we see it as* an entire process of self-emptying *instead of a dramatic three hours on the cross. For some Christian denominations the first 30 years of Jesus' life mean nothing: his teaching can be ignored. It's just those last three hours. I don't mean to be disrespectful, but it amounts to "get that blood" instead of a whole life of self-emptying.*

1. Richard encourages us to see this path that Jesus followed in letting go of the false self and giving birth to the true self (or universal self) as something to be emulated. He acknowledges that this path isn't attractive to Western Christians. What would it actually mean "to let go of the false self" and to fully embrace the natural cycles of life and death?

3. If it's attractive to you and is, perhaps, the way you live, what makes it so?

2. What is it about this path that makes it unattractive to Western Christians?

OPTION 3: LEVELS OF CONSCIOUSNESS

As you listen to Richard teaching and interacting, you'll notice that on a number of occasions he speaks about the process of human development that moves us as individuals and as a culture through a number of levels of consciousness, from magical (transactional), through mythical, rational and pluralistic, and finally to mystical or non-dual. We are focusing on this understanding of human and cultural development here because this approach is so influential in Richard's thinking and teaching. It also leads to a reflection on what Richard refers to as *alternative orthodoxy*.

Richard's reflection on levels of consciousness began with a question from Joe:

> *There is a certain attractiveness to the crucifixion and the death of Christ being the just result. Justice is now here to pay for the evil or transgressions that humanity engaged in before. I can see where the majority view was well received.*

Richard responds:

> *I've been influenced in the last 10 years so much by things like Spiral Dynamics, Integral Theory and levels of consciousness. The early level of consciousness is the magical level; what I call the transactional level. It's also the ego level, what I call the quid pro quo. It really doesn't understand restorative justice. It's only retributive justice: quid pro quo or tit for tat. That's where all of our minds are. Look at your 11-year-old: they want* quid pro quo. *"Follow the rules." "You said!" We all go through that level of consciousness, and culture itself did too. It couldn't understand restorative justice*

> *in the 11th century, namely, that God, in fact, justifies us by loving us more, not by punitiveness. That didn't even make sense.*

> *You put it very well, Joe. There's a certain level of attractiveness to "paying a price"— quid pro quo. It does satisfy an early level of the mammalian brain. Things are justified. The playing field is leveled. The thing we Christians believe is that the gospel goes far beyond that: the Doctrine of Mercy and Grace has nothing to do with* quid pro quo.

Later in the conversation Richard returns with further reflection on levels of consciousness:

> *As a culture we are at the pluralistic level. That's why so many things that were understood at the magical and mythical level don't make sense to us anymore. I don't want to throw them out. I want to ask how you raise them up and see that they are truer than ever. Once we get to the highest non-dual or mystical level, we really understand the transaction of love—the transformational power of love. I don't want to throw out any of these doctrines or dogmas; let's find out what they really mean.*

> *That's why we use the term* alternative orthodoxy. *We're still concerned about being orthodox, but what so many people call orthodox is childhood conditioning passing for orthodoxy. It doesn't help because when they go off to college at the rational level of consciousness where it doesn't make sense anymore, they throw out the baby with the bath water. That's why agnosticism and atheism are largely a child of Christianity. If you go to formerly Christian nations you find a high degree of agnostics and atheists.*

1. Through Richard's teaching we can begin to see that concepts like traditional atonement are not only a product of historical process but also a reflection of the development of human consciousness. When have you been aware of your own journey of consciousness being influential in your beliefs and practices as a person of faith?

2. Richard talks about the move from *quid pro quo* (tit for tat) thinking to the gospel of grace as one example of a development of higher consciousness. A cultural expression of that is in the shift from retributive justice to restorative justice. When have you been aware of either a personal or cultural move from *quid pro quo* thinking to something that reflects the transformative power of love?

OPTION 4: ALERT TO ATONEMENT THEOLOGY

Atonement Theology can be as unnoticed as the air we breath. Its presence and language has become so familiar that we can be unaware of it until a circumstance or an individual actually draws our attention to it.

In Handel's *Messiah,* notice the presence of atonement theology:

> Surely He hath borne our griefs, and carried our sorrows!
> He was wounded for our transgressions;
> He was bruised for our iniquities;
> the chastisement of our peace was upon Him.
> And with His stripes we are healed.
>
> All we like sheep have gone astray;
> we have turned every one to his own way.
> And the Lord hath laid on Him the iniquity of us all.
>
> He was cut off out of the land of the living;
> for the transgression of Thy people was He stricken.

Here is one example of hymns in the Episcopal *Hymnal 1982* that reflect atonement theology:

> Cross of Jesus, cross of sorrow, where the blood of Christ was shed,
> perfect Man on thee did suffer, perfect God on thee has bled!
>
> Here the King of all the ages, throned in light ere worlds could be,
> robed in mortal flesh is dying, crucified by sin for me.
>
> O mysterious condescending! O abandonment sublime!
> Very God himself is bearing all the sufferings of time!
>
> Cross of Jesus, cross of sorrow, where the blood of Christ was shed,
> perfect Man on thee did suffer, perfect God on thee has bled!

Words: William J. Sparrow-Simpson (1860–1952)

We see atonement theology reflected in The Book of Common Prayer:

> All glory be to thee
> Almighty God, our heavenly Father,
> who of thy tender mercy
> didst give thine only Son Jesus Christ
> to suffer death upon the cross
> for our redemption;
> who made there,
> by his one oblation
> of himself once offered,
> a full, perfect and sufficient sacrifice,
> oblation and satisfaction
> for the sins of the whole world;
> and did institute,
> and in his holy gospel command us to continue,
> a perpetual memory of that his precious death,
> until his coming again.

Eucharistic Prayer I (Rite I of Holy Eucharist, p. 334)

1. When have you been aware of the presence of atonement theology either in roadside signs or in Sunday worship?

2. What hymns and prayers do you know that give expression to an alternative orthodoxy that speaks the truth in a way that resonates with your beliefs?

OPTION 5: SHAPED BY WILLFULNESS; YEARNING FOR WILLINGNESS

Doug asks:

Isn't it inevitable that experience is going to have to teach us that quid pro quo doesn't work?

Richard responds:

We've been shaped much more by American culture. We like will-power religion: "I can do whatever I need to do." The language of the scriptures and the mystics and saints is not the language of willfulness but willingness—the language of surrender. Jesus surrenders to his passion. He's not steering the whole thing, he's surrendering to what has to happen, what's inevitable. That's a very different language than "pulling up by my own bootstraps"! We are so formed by that notion that we pretend it's the gospel. Christian preachers talk that way: "You can do it! You can do anything you want!"

In biblical theory that's pure heresy, yet you can get away talking that way in a pulpit. Willfulness appeals to the egocentric, low-level self. It looks like winners win. What the gospel is saying is losers win. We should all be happy about that because it includes all of us. That's why I wrote the book Falling Upward. *I wanted to show that you've got to go through that falling experience. Your initial self-created game for superiority has to disappoint you, has to fall apart on some level or you never get to the second half of life, which is the gospel possibility.*

1. This is a huge condemnation by Richard of the meaning of religion within American culture. And it's an alarming description of the consequence to individuals of that cultural reality. This conversation about surrender and falling into the second half of life has to be one of the hardest conversations for privileged North Americans! Listen with care. Speak with courage. How is this characterization of religion in America borne out in your experience and observation?

2. What has America lost as a result of the appropriation of religion that Richard is describing?

3. How has this tension between willfulness and willingness been lived out in your life? Where do you find yourself now?

OPTION 6: A DEEP CONCERN
FOR THE GENERATIONS TO COME

Suzanne and Jennifer give voice to their passion for ensuring that these insights that come under the title *alternative orthodoxy* will be available to and desired by their children and grandchildren.

Suzanne puts it this way:

> *I hope that my son and his generation will not have to fight the fight that I'm fighting now. It took me a while to get to this because I was trying to remain loyal. Finally, through years of reading and being open to other ways of thinking, I realized this is no threat at all: I can hang on to these other things. I don't want the next generation to have to undergo that. Maybe if we do our part in introducing this to them early on, telling them, "This is important, but so is this:* God is a loving God!"

And Jennifer adds:

> *Something I've seen in working with adults in education are grandparents who see that their adult children aren't baptizing the grandchildren, so the grandparents do it. And it's not out of love, but out of fear, fear that if this child does not have water poured on its head and a ritualistic formula said exactly this way, then if the child dies he or she will go to hell. That to me says so much about what your image of God is. It's so important to communicate to our children, to our grandchildren a different image of God than what I had. I had the cosmic attendance-taker keeping track of my sins and of my attendance at mass instead of a God who from the get-go planned to come and meet us where we are.*

Richard responds briefly:

> *We've discovered—and I'm sure you as educators know this—it's not what parents say, it's what they're excited about. If you talk about this in an excited way, it's sold. It takes.*

1. We are in a time in mainline Christianity when participation in the life of the congregation at all age levels, but especially at younger ages, is in dramatic decline. Many congregations have neither children nor younger adults participating in the life of their faith community, so this issue raised by Suzanne and Jennifer really matters. *Theology* matters. Why would people stick around to hear about a God who is keeping track of your sins and your attendance at church? Richard reminds us that genuine excitement about something that really matters makes a difference to those who are learning and seeking. What do you think about all this?

2. Is it too late for Christianity to recover from its history of bad theology?

3. What do you intend to do in terms of the spiritual and faith-formation of the generations to come, especially the ones in whose lives you have an influence?

OPTION 7: A BIBLICAL HYMN OF AT-ONE-MENT

Richard states:

> *The Early Franciscan School of which St. Bonaventure and John Duns Scotus were both preeminent philosophers, both emphasize the hymns at the beginning of Colossians and Ephesians and the Prologue to John's Gospel as expressions of a nonviolent atonement theology.*

And so we turn to the hymn near the beginning of Paul's letter to the brothers and sisters in Colossae:

Colossians 1:15-20

15 He is the image of the invisible God, the firstborn of all creation;

16 for in him all things in heaven and on earth were created, things visible and invisible, whether thrones or dominions or rulers or powers—all things have been created through him and for him.

17 He himself is before all things, and in him all things hold together.

18 He is the head of the body, the church; he is the beginning, the firstborn from the dead, so that he might come to have first place in everything.

19 For in him all the fullness of God was pleased to dwell,

20 and through him God was pleased to reconcile to himself all things, whether on earth or in heaven, by making peace through the blood of his cross.

In his book, *Things Hidden: Scripture as Spirituality*, Richard Rohr writes a short exegesis on the hymn at the beginning of Colossians:

> Jesus, Scotus said, was not "necessary" to solve any problem whatsoever—he was no mopping-up exercise after the fact—but a pure and gracious declaration of the primordial truth from the very beginning which was called the doctrine of "the primacy of Christ."
>
> The Incarnation of God, in Jesus, gives us the living "icon of the invisible God" (Colossians I:15), who is the template for all else (I:16), who reconciles all things in himself (I:17), who is the headmaster in a cosmic body that follows after him (I:18). If I may use a contemporary image: Jesus is the "hologram" for all that is happening in a constant and repetitive universe (I:19). He is the pattern for all. He does what we also must do, which is why he says, "follow me."
>
> The human Jesus, in other words, is God's preemptive statement to humanity about history and the soul. This "Word of God"—all distilled and focused in one visible life—which is "secretly" Divine but overtly human. Sort of like us!

Let me summarize: *Whatever happens to Jesus is what must and will happen to the soul*: incarnation, an embodied life of ordinariness and hiddenness, initiation, trial, faith, death, surrender, resurrection and return to God. Such is the Christ pattern that we all share in, either joyfully and trustfully (heaven), or unwillingly and resentfully (hell).

Things Hidden: Scripture as Spirituality,
Richard Rohr (Cincinnati, OH:
St Anthony Messenger Press, 2008, p. 198)

Take the scripture passage and Richard's exegesis of it as you would another passage and reflection in a Bible study, finding:
- the parts of it that speak strongly to you
- the elements that unsettle you
- the questions that arise and provoke further thought and conversation

OPTION 8: PERSONAL REFLECTION

(for use following the session)

Following the session you will continue to think about issues raised both on the DVD and in your small group. This suggestion for journaling is offered to support you in continuing your reflection beyond the session time.

1. You may not have had time to complete all the options in the group study time. As you have time, take the opportunity for personal reflection on the ones that you missed or the ones that were really engaging and to which you now want to return on your own.

2. You will have seen that Richard Rohr is convicted by his calling as a Franciscan, by his profound immersion in the reality of God, and by his capacity to bring together theological issues with the deepest concerns of human life. Because of this, he is a remarkably compelling and inspiring teacher. What was it from all the things that you heard him say that most stayed with you? Reflect on why that matters to you. What questions would you like to ask Richard?

Because Richard Rohr introduces us to an alternative to traditional orthodoxy, we close each session with a prayer that gives expression to orthodoxy while also allowing room for a contemporary theology.

Prayer of Alcuin
(8th Century Celtic)

> Give us, O Lord, we pray,
>   firm faith,
>   unwavering hope,
>   a passion for justice.
>
> Pour into our hearts
>   the Spirit of Wisdom and Understanding,
>   the Spirit of Counsel and Spiritual Strength,
>   the Spirit of Knowledge and True Compassion,
>   the Spirit of Wonder in all Your Works.
>
> Light Eternal,
>   shine in our hearts;
> Power Eternal,
>   deliver us from evil;
> Wisdom Eternal,
>   scatter the darkness of our ignorance;
> Might Eternal,
>   have mercy on us.
>
> Grant that we may ever seek your face
>   with all our heart, soul and strength.
> And in your infinite mercy
>   bring us at last to the fullness of your presence
>   where we shall behold your glory
>   and live your promised joys.
>
> In the name of Jesus,
>   our body and blood,
>   our life and our nourishment.
>
> *Amen.*

SESSION | 2

Eco-Spirituality

BEFORE THE SESSION

Many participants like to come to the group conversation after considering individually some of the issues that will be raised. The following five reflective activities are intended to open your mind, memories and emotions regarding some aspects of this session's topic. Use the space provided here to note your reflections.

1. When you hear the term *eco-spirituality*, what comes to mind for you?

2. Based on your reading and various media presentations, what are you noticing these days about the global ecological crisis? What feelings does this engender in you? How do your spiritual practices address this growing crisis?

3. In the time before the next session, find an opportunity to go to a place that allows you to practice "an open-eyed reverencing of reality."

4. Think about the way your congregational life is structured and managed. Look for ways that it encourages transformation of human life toward a deeper consciousness of God's presence in all things. Look for ways that it maintains the status quo and encourages dualistic thinking (either/or, winners and losers, for me or against me) rather than mystical consciousness.

5. Go to the Closing for this session where you will find "The Canticle of Brother Sun and Sister Moon" by St. Francis (p. 48). Find times during the week to read this aloud or in silence. Allow the reading to carry you into the worldview of St. Francis, who granted animals, elements and planets subjectivity, respect and mutuality by calling them *brothers* and *sisters*.

The theme of this study is "Embracing An Alternative Orthodoxy." You have come together as a group, ready to uncover some responses to this question: What are the dynamics of alternative orthodoxy in the second decade of the 21st century?

In the course of this session, you will hear Richard Rohr singing the praises of these kinds of small group gatherings in churches as a sign of alternative community that will be critical for the future of faith and especially for the development of contemplative consciousness.

Take a moment to share with one another what gift you see in this kind of gathering for your journey of evolving awareness.

OPTION 1: INTRODUCTION TO ECO-SPIRITUALITY

Before you watch to the DVD, talk together about what you understand by the term *eco-spirituality*. Allow these questions to inform your conversation:

1. What do you understand to be the connection between ecology and spirituality?

2. When have you witnessed the bond between ecological concern and spirituality being positive for creation, including humanity? Conversely, when have you witnessed it being less positive for the creation?

3. How is your knowledge of God related to your relationship with the environment?

> God wants us to be
> good stewards + mindful
> of the environment.

Take a moment to write your own definition of *eco-spirituality* in the space provided here:

Before selecting from the following options, *watch the entire portion of the DVD for Session 2.*

OPTION 2: WORDS AT THE MEETING PLACE OF ECO-SPIRITUALITY AND ALTERNATIVE ORTHODOXY

Two things to notice from the presentation:

1. Richard is introducing us to *alternative orthodoxy* through the theme of *eco-spirituality*; we are learning about both matters simultaneously.

2. As we listen to Richard's teaching, we realize that he has a way of considering eco-spirituality and alternative orthodoxy that comes with their own vocabularies. To the right are 12 key words and phrases from his presentation and discussion. Before going on to the next section, take a look at this list. As you do so, consider:

   • Which words or phrases stand out for you personally from your initial listening to Richard's teaching?

   • What is it about those words or phrases that attracts you?

   • What personal insights would you now add to your earlier reflections on the relationship between ecology and spirituality?

Key Words:

— Individualism

— Participatory Universe

— Incarnation

— Cosmology

— Mysticism

— The Contemplative Mind

— Silence

— Creation, the First Bible

— Franciscan Worldview

— Evolution

— Transformation of Consciousness

— Transcend and Include

OPTION 3: THE MOUTH THAT ROHR'D

In the course of his initial presentation, we hear Richard Rohr speak boldly about many issues of both alternative orthodoxy and eco-spirituality. You will remember much of what he said. Here is a selection to inspire group conversation:

Richard on individualism:

> The single biggest heresy that allows us to misinterpret the scriptural tradition is individualism, revealed now in the problem we are facing with earth care, with sustainability, with animal species dying off. We became so anthropocentric that God cared not about the new heaven and the new earth, but "just us" and, as I said, not very many of us. That's what happens when you go down the track of individualism and lose the mystical level of perception.

Richard on the Franciscan worldview:

> Francis is the first recorded Western Christian who granted animals, elements and planets subjectivity, respect and mutuality by calling them brothers and sisters. It's a participatory universe that Francis expresses with wind, with fire, with Sun and Moon; the whole universe is a participatory experience.

Richard on incarnation:

> You'd think that Christianity would have got incarnation early and first because we're the only religion that concretely believes that the Divine took on flesh. No one else claims that the Divine became a human being. But much of our history has been ex-carnation, that is, how to get out of the world. We didn't get incarnation except in a very narrow sense. And now we're paying the price for it: the huge dying off of species and the pollution of the earth.

Richard on cosmology:

> Cosmology is the new name for theology. Like no other generations, we know the extent of the mystery of the universe. We can give a date for its beginning. Ninety-nine percent of it is emptiness, is silence, is space and is darkness—all the things we avoid, run from and deny as important. God created a universe that is mostly dark, empty, silent space! Does that have anything to teach consciousness? Until you can honor silence you don't know how to interpret the particles inside the spaces. They have no meaning except in the relationship between them.

Richard on mysticism:

The emphasis on the individual reflects the lack of the mystical level. Mysticism is always about more and more connecting. You realize that you are participating in something bigger and you are part of a mystery. You wonder if the one thing we all share in common across all religions is that we've all stood on this same earth and we've all looked up at this same Brother Sun, Sister Moon. Could it be that the mystery is already encapsulated there?

Richard on the "first Bible":

The early Franciscans called creation "The First Bible." If you murdered and mangled and manipulated and did not attend to or respect the First Bible, the assumption was that you would murder, mangle and manipulate the second Bible. You could make the case that the Bible has done as much damage in human history as it has done good.

Richard on religion and ecology:

I can't give up on religion. Religion grants inherent sacrality, inherent holiness, goodness, value and worthiness to the material world. No religion does that better in theory than Christianity. But we individualized it—we pulled it into our private human selves, and we didn't have the mature eyes to see that it isn't only I that have materiality, but my dog has it too and those trees have it. They share in that same material universe that I share. It creates a truly global spirituality of which humanity is capable. We're not just capable of it; if we don't get it, we're in trouble.

1. Richard Rohr is one of the most widely read Christian theologians in North America today. He has a large and enthusiastic following. As you can see and hear, he doesn't mince words. Many folks would say, "This is exactly the kind of bold and prophetic leadership we need in Christianity today!" What do you think?

2. From the various things you have heard Richard say, what one thing would you take and share with friends? Try putting that into your own words and saying it to friends in this circle of learning right now.

OPTION 4: WHAT ARE WE TO DO?

Jennifer asks Richard: "So what are we to do?"

Suzanne speaks of how, when it comes to ecological crises such as the oil spill in the Gulf, she is torn between "mopping up" and "changing the mindset":

> *If we get into the mopping up, it's just a vicious cycle of fixing the problems they generated as opposed to following the vision of St. Francis.*

In his response Richard proposes three ways of moving forward in deepening our eco-spiritual consciousness while addressing our theological dysfunction:

> *A lot of us have been saying in recent years that much of our teaching is unlearning. That's why I resort to the teaching of contemplation so much because contemplation in practice is a daily exercise in self-emptying, in detaching, in unlearning your learned patterns.*

> *We have to grant a kind of humility to religion again because it hasn't been very humble.*

> *We do well to emphasize an optimistic worldview. We need something to be for much more than something to be against. You need a great big positive vision to seduce the soul out. To simply operate out of pure praise, glory and love—that's a higher level of motivation, but one that doesn't easily come our way.*

1. How would you apply these strategies to your situation both personally and communally?

2. What other strategies would you offer to move us beyond the dire situation that Richard earlier describes?

OPTION 5: DEVELOPING CONTEMPLATIVE SEEING

Raymond recalls times when he has been surrounded by the awesomeness of nature. There he notices the sublime reality that we humans are just one of millions of species on this planet and not necessarily here forever. At such times the truth of God's everywhere presence in creation settles into him.

In response Richard reflects on contemplative seeing, describing it as:

> *An open-eyed reverencing of reality—seeing that it all has value without label, without functional purpose. Experiencing universal connection, reverence and awe, I walk into that massive canyon, the rock soaring above. I am humbled. It was here long before me and it will be here long after. I'm walking through it this day. Who am I to think that I name it; perhaps it's naming me!*

1. When are you captivated by the awe of creation in the way Raymond and Richard describe?

2. What are your practices for developing your contemplative seeing?

3. What mystical insights have come to you through contemplative seeing?

OPTION 6: INCARNATION, GRACE AND EVOLUTION

When someone introduces the topic of evolution into the conversation, Richard seizes the opportunity to use it to further illuminate the potential of incarnation fully realized:

> *You would have thought if we had understood incarnation, Christians should have been on the front lines of understanding evolution, because grace is inherent to creation. We're the ones who believe God created* all things, *and yet grace was still extrinsic to the universe. So evolution was not in our natural understanding.*

> *Francis took incarnation to its logical conclusion. That's what makes us a minority position inside the church. Even though mainline Catholicism was sacramental and supposedly saw the physical world as a doorway into the spiritual world, by and large most Catholics also saw grace as extrinsic to the universe: God who occasionally visited and gave you grace. The light didn't shine from inside! That's why we weren't prepared for evolution—and even fought it.*

1. How do you see it: God's grace intrinsic to the universe, including the whole journey of evolution, or extrinsic and occasionally granted?

2. What does evolution tell you about God?

OPTION 7: TRANSFORMATION AND CHURCH STRUCTURES

Doug acknowledges his excitement at everything that Richard is saying, but then wonders as a parish priest:

> *How do you get people to calm down enough to understand what contemplation really is, to undergo the transformation of consciousness that enables them to look at their dog and say, "This is a fellow creature"?*

In his response Richard moves us into an examination of the insufficiency of current church structures:

> *We need structures that encourage people at the mystical level, because that is the level that Jesus is at. If you want to understand Jesus, you've got to have an openness to it or you pull him down into dualistic thinking: either/or, for me or against me.*

> *People come to church with the expectation not to be changed; it's to be told again what they already agree with. The structure itself doesn't lend itself to transformation. The future isn't in the large congregation because it doesn't come with the expectation of transformation, grace and growth. It doesn't come with "beginner's mind."*

1. In what ways is your church's structure facilitating or inhibiting change and transformation?

2. How badly do you want to be transformed into the Way of Jesus? What might it cost you?

3. What kind of faith community activity and structure would support you in your desire for transformation?

OPTION 8: TRANSCEND AND INCLUDE

In response to Doug's weariness with the extent of anxiety at the future of the church and his observation that there is more obvious spiritual discipline in spiritually-focused groups outside the church than inside, Richard introduces Ken Wilber's principle, *Transcend and Include*. He adds his own formulation when he says, "If you have transcended, you can include."

As a way of making this principle even more concrete, Richard presents the way that Francis modeled it:

> *In 13th century Italy, Catholicism was the only game in town, so Francis found a way to survive inside it but did it very differently. He moved outside the walls of Assisi and he didn't fight the Bishop and priests inside the walls. He would still go to those churches on feast days and occasions, but he did it differently.*

Richard sums up the conversation in naming one of the principles of his Center for Action and Contemplation in Albuquerque:

> *The best criticism of the bad is the practice of the better.*

1. What does living the principle of "Transcend and Include" look like for you and for others who share your frustrations, concerns and visions within the current structures of church?

2. In what ways are you actually living "the practice of the better" as a positive way of moving beyond that which needs to be left behind?

OPTION 9: PERSONAL REFLECTION

(for use following the session)

Following the session you will continue to think about issues raised both on the DVD and in your small group. This suggestion for journaling is offered to support you in continuing your reflection beyond the session time.

1. You may not have had time in the session to address all the topics. Go back on your own to the ones you missed and reflect personally on the issues addressed there.

2. How will you honor and advance the contemplative part of your life? There are so many opportunities: yoga, centering prayer, Buddhist mindfulness, meditation of many kinds, chanting, worship in the style of Taize, spiritual direction, Celtic walking, healing touch and so much more. Consider that there may be merit in inviting other members of the group—or of your congregation—into an intentional practice of contemplative formation.

Because Richard Rohr introduces us to an alternative to traditional orthodoxy, we close each session with a prayer that gives expression to orthodoxy while also allowing room for a contemporary theology.

You have heard Richard make reference to the Canticle of St. Francis, which is presented here as a prayer for your closing:

Canticle of Brother Sun and Sister Moon
St. Francis of Assisi

Most high, all powerful, all good Lord!
All praise is Yours, all glory, all honor and all blessing.

To You, alone, Most High, do they belong.
No mortal lips are worthy to pronounce Your name.

Be praised, my Lord, through all Your creatures,
especially through my lord Brother Sun, who brings the day;
You give light through him.
And he is beautiful and radiant in all his splendor!
Of You, Most High, he bears the likeness.

Be praised, my Lord, through Sister Moon and the stars in the heavens.
You have made them bright, precious and beautiful.

Be praised, my Lord, through Brothers Wind and Air,
and clouds and storms, and all the weather,
through which You give Your creatures sustenance.

Be praised, my Lord, through Sister Water;
she is very useful, and humble, and precious, and pure.

Be praised, my Lord, through Brother Fire,
through whom You brighten the night.
He is beautiful and cheerful, and powerful and strong.

Be praised, my Lord, through our sister Mother Earth,
who feeds us and rules us, and produces various fruits with colored flowers and herbs.

Be praised, my Lord, through those who forgive for love of You;
through those who endure sickness and trial.

Happy are those who endure in peace by You, Most High, they will be crowned.

Be praised, my Lord, through our sister Bodily Death,
from whose embrace no living person can escape.
Woe to those who die in mortal sin!
Happy those she finds doing Your most holy will.
The second death can do no harm to them.

Praise and bless my Lord, and give thanks, and serve Him with great humility.

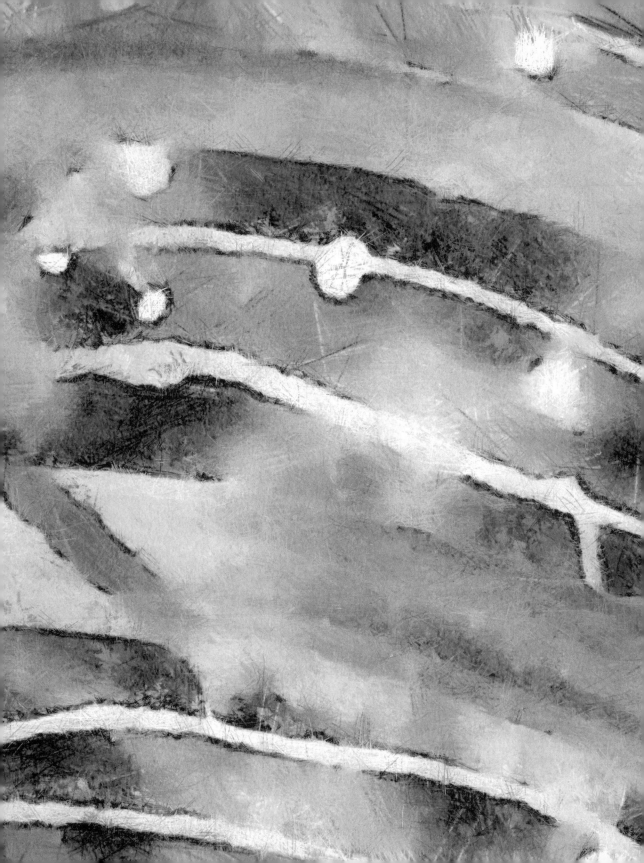

SESSION | 3

THE COSMIC CHRIST

BEFORE THE SESSION

Many participants like to come to the group conversation after considering individually some of the issues that will be raised. The following five reflective activities are intended to open your mind, memories and emotions regarding some aspects of this session's topic. Use the space provided here to note your reflections.

1. Take a blank page of paper and draw on it two large intersecting circles. In one circle write *Jesus* and in the other *Christ*. In each circle write the words and phrases that you associate with each word. In the area where the two circles intersect, write words and phrases that you see the two words holding in common.

2. What season of the church year are you in right now? Advent? Christmas? Epiphany/Ordinary Time? Lent? Easter? the Season of Creation? the Season after Pentecost/Ordinary Time? How does living in that season color your relationship with the Christ who permeates all creation?

3. In this session Fr. Rohr will call our attention to five passages of scripture which the first Franciscans emphasized as they lived into the understanding that Christ existed from the beginning of creation:
   • Colossians 1
   • Ephesians 1
   • John 1:1-18
   • 1 John 1
   • Hebrews 1

   Read one or two of these passages, appreciating them as expressions of the materialization of God in the first incarnation billions of years ago at the big bang.

4. In a hymnal, find the section containing hymns on the theme of *Jesus* and *Christ*. Scan the selections there, finding lines that appeal to you as you reflect on the significance of those two names. Notice ways that hymn writers have their own distinctive—and sometimes contradictory—theologies woven into their lyrics.

5. If the Christ mystery has been present in the creation from the beginning, then it has been accessed by an incredible diversity of humans over hundreds of thousands of years. As Christians, our identity is shaped by the particular manifestation of Christ consciousness 2000 years ago in Jesus. What do you claim as a follower of Jesus Christ?

In the course of this session, you will hear Richard make reference several times to measuring your treatment of someone who is doing what might be considered a menial task. "How you love anything is how you love everything," he says. The way that you honor and respect the members of this study group is the way that you honor and respect people in any of your life circumstances. A study group of this kind—where you are respectfully engaging members of your faith community in things that matter to you deeply—provides a setting not only for acquiring knowledge and insight, but also for sharpening your capacity for conscious compassion and sacred accompaniment.

Notice how the life of this group supports your desire to be truly living with the mind of Christ. What can you do together to remind you that this is what you are mostly here for? Could you light a candle? say a prayer? speak together about how you matter to one another? share food?

Before selecting from the following options, *watch the entire portion of the DVD for Session 3.*

OPTION 1: TOUCHING THE COSMIC CHRIST

You've heard Richard Rohr talk about his understanding of the Cosmic Christ, a key element of alternative orthodoxy that is an aspect of the legacy of the early Franciscans. It may be a challenge for you to really grasp all that is intended by the term *Cosmic Christ*, but the presence of your group and its process can support you in coming to terms with this theological perspective. Discuss the four questions below as you work together to understand this concept. For each question, there are key words related to an aspect of this theology:

1. *Key Words:* the big bang—the first incarnation—the birth of the Christ mystery—the interplanetary Divine

   What are the implications of saying that the birth of Christ occurred at the moment of the creation of the material universe?

2. *Key Words:* a second incarnation—2000 years ago—an exemplar—for Christians—the mystery of God

   What does it mean to use the two words *Jesus* and *Christ* together, not as two names for Jesus but as an expression of a mystical reality?

3. *Key Words:* Eucharist—elemental incarnation in a material universe—"Oh my God, I am the body of Christ!"

How might you now experience the Eucharist differently as you consider these insights about the Cosmic Christ?

4. *Key Words:* Nothing is secular—grace indwelling—mountains as cathedrals—Divine image

In unitive consciousness, how you love anything is how you love everything. How might your life be transformed if you embraced the Franciscan vision found in Richard's teaching in this session?

OPTION 2: PAUL GETS IT!

Richard Rohr encourages us to see the gift that Paul is to us as we struggle to grasp this vision of the Cosmic Christ. Have someone read the following indented text aloud in the group, then enter into a conversation guided by the questions that follow:

> *The personal incarnation happened 2000 years ago, we believe as Christians, which is Jesus. They became so infatuated with this person of Jesus that very quickly they seemed to call him the Christ, although there's no evidence that he ever called himself that. The scriptural evidence is that it was Paul who got it. Paul gets it because Paul knew Jesus Christ the way we do. He never knew Jesus in the flesh. He hardly ever quotes him and yet he talks with such authority, such certitude. He met the Christ mystery and until you know that, you do not understand the mystic Paul. He is in love with this Christ mystery, which is the same Jesus Christ that you and I meet.*

> *So when we introduce people to Jesus without the rest of the incarnation—the Christ—we end up with a moralistic religion. Moralism takes over whenever you don't have mysticism. You will become more moralistic the less it touches upon unitive consciousness. The Christ is something you know mystically. When I say mystically, I mean experientially. Whatever happened to Paul on the Damascus Road, he knew experientially some universal meaning to this Jesus figure—and he universalized from that. His most common single phrase in his authentic letters is* in Christo—*in Christ. That's his code word for this understanding.*

> *We are living inside this incarnation. We are the Christ too! He's not denying Jesus Christ. Jesus Christ is the* holon, *the exemplar of the whole, the stand-in for everybody. We can't fall in love with concepts, energies, ideas and forces. You're not going to give your life for a force. As 1 John says, we need someone we can see, and touch, and look into his or her eyes, and relate to. Persons love persons. That pulls our soul out of itself.*

1. When have you "experienced" the Christ mystery in the way that Paul seems to have done?

2. Paul and Richard would have us see that we are living inside an incarnation—in Christ—but we don't fall in love with a concept. What do you fall in love with in such a way that your soul is enlivened?

OPTION 3: OUR GOD MAY BE TOO SMALL

If we follow Franciscan orthodoxy, which teaches that Christ is incarnated in all creation right from the big bang, then sooner or later we have to deal with the matter of other civilizations, cultures, traditions, revelations and religions in a way that honors the Christ mystery that is incarnate in the immense diversity of creation. Have someone read aloud Richard's reflections on this matter and then discuss the questions that follow:

> Jesus is the personal personification of the eternal Christ mystery, but the Christ mystery was already available to the Stone Age people, to the Persians, to the Mayans, to the so-called barbarians and pagans. These were not "throw away people!" That's what you came down to if you were Roman Catholic: God was waiting for the Pope to appear and everything else was throwaway. Imagine that! You'd have to say that this is a petty God, a small God.

> If we don't balance out Jesus with Christ, our very theology is going to become a very limited worldview. It ends up being in competition with other world religions instead of a vision that is so big, so cosmic that it includes everything and everybody.

> When you return to a Trinitarian notion of God, it opens up interfaith dialogue, because you admit God is formless. You admit God is energy and spirit, which is the Holy Spirit. Suddenly we have all kinds of levels for dialogue. What happened when we pulled Jesus out of the Christ mystery and out of the Trinity? We overplayed the Jesus card apart from who Jesus really is. That made us unable to talk to Hindus and Buddhists, to respect the Jewish roots of this very Jesus.

> Jesus then becomes in competition with Muhammad or Buddha. It becomes a personality issue: "Do you like Jesus. Well, if you don't like Jesus, well then God doesn't like you!" Come on! The question is, "Do you like the Christ Mystery?" I can see your answer to that in the way you walk down the street and the way you respect the person at the checkout counter. There are some Hindus that like the Christ mystery much better than a lot of Roman Catholics, Evangelicals, Lutherans and Episcopalians. I'm happy to be Christian, but that doesn't put me in competition or a race with the other world religions to prove that I'm better.

> We're not trying to be rebels anymore; we're not trying to be reactionary or heretics. We're just trying to be honest about our experience. And that ability we now have to be honest about our experience is making us ready for an adult Christianity, for an adult notion of what's really happening, without throwing out Jesus. You'll go back and fall in love with Jesus more than ever before, but now you'll recognize that this Jesus is not just the Savior of my soul, but he's the naming of the very direction of history—the Alpha and Omega—this perfected humanity that he reveals in one moment of time and where we are all being seduced toward.

1. In a creation of such awesome diversity, where the Christ mystery is available to all, what is it that gives you your Christian identity? What do you claim as a follower of Jesus Christ?

3. What would you now like to talk about with people from other faith traditions in your community?

2. Richard has a way of provoking more good questions even while answering the earlier ones. What questions would you like to ask him as part of deepening into a more adult Christianity?

OPTION 4: A LOT TO WRAP OUR HEADS AROUND!

For many who are listening to Richard, what he is proposing is nothing less than a shift in worldview at the deepest level. He helps us to appreciate the challenging journey of transformation by reminding us several times of the levels of consciousness that Ken Wilber has articulated: *archaic—magical—mythical—rational—pluralistic—mystical (non-dual).*

Jennifer gives voice to the kind of challenge involved in this intentional movement toward non-dual living:

> *It's hard for me to wrap my head around it. It goes back to Richard's definition of* faith: *the dichotomy of not knowing and knowing. A lot of it's my upbringing in the scientific method and the emphasis on proof. I think that's why the historical Jesus is so attractive at the rational level because there are things you can know and things you can understand. Yet, at the same time we don't call ourselves Jesus-ians! We call ourselves Christ-ians. So we really need to understand what it is to be Christian and to understand Christ and God in all creation from the beginning. It didn't just begin with "I"— incarnated here on earth. It's a lot to wrap your head around!*

Richard acknowledges Jennifer's observation and hints at what the process of transformation might look like:

> *Your mind, your prayers, your songs, your reading of the scripture will almost have to readjust for two years; but then you'll see it everywhere. Once you see it, you'll know this isn't my idea. It's there, but no one told me to pay attention to it.*

1. Where do you find yourself in this process of growing consciousness? In what ways does Jennifer give voice to your thoughts and feelings?

2. Richard is hinting at a classic process of spiritual practice and discernment: "putting on a new mind" as Paul would say. What are your practices for opening yourself to a new way of seeing that would transform your life completely?

OPTION 5: MOVING LIBERALS ALONG

Doug makes an observation that holds a mirror up to liberals, the very people who are likely to be using this study:

> *There's a liberal temptation to focus so much on the historic Jesus until we can say X, Y and Z about the historic Jesus. When you get the cosmic aspect it blows open both the conservative and liberal paradigm.*

Richard responds:

> *It critiques the liberal just as much as the conservative, because neither of us understands the Christ very well. Ken Wilber has pointed out in describing the level of consciousness that the downside of the pluralistic level—where most liberals are—is that they are so in love with pluralism that they hate any notion of hierarchy. When you go to the mystical level (the Cosmic Christ level), then you really appreciate hierarchy. Then you have a new criterion for critiquing the liberal just as much as the conservative. Liberals tend to be trapped because they are just smart enough to dismiss everyone below as superstitious and ridiculous and everyone above them as falsely religious in their mystical silliness. They stay there, many of them, the rest of their lives and can be just as dogmatic, authoritarian and dualistic while thinking they are not. You can really appreciate what Wilber calls hierarchy. Yes, there are things that are still needy of analysis and critique—not dismissal—and that includes the liberal mind, the pluralistic mind, which thinks that the goal of history is pluralism. The goal of history is union with God which honors pluralism but doesn't get trapped there as an end in itself.*

1. Where do you find yourself in this analysis?

2. How might churches with a liberal bias encourage their members to experience the goal of history as union with God?

OPTION 6: PAYING ATTENTION BIBLICALLY

Richard calls attention to five passages of scripture that were emphasized by the first Franciscans as they lived into the reality of the Christ that existed from the beginning of creation:

- Colossians 1
- Ephesians 1
- John 1:1-18
- 1 John 1
- Hebrews 1

These hymns all say that the Christ existed from all eternity. The Cosmic Christ is "totally biblical, but no one told us to pay attention to it."

Choose one of the five passages listed above and read it through the lens of Richard's teaching in this session. What do you notice that you hadn't seen before when reading these passages? What questions remain?

OPTION 7: PERSONAL REFLECTION

(for use following the session)

Following the session you will continue to think about issues raised both on the DVD and in your small group. This suggestion for journaling is offered to support you in continuing your reflection beyond the session time.

1. You may not have had time in the session to address all the topics. Go back on your own to the ones you missed and reflect personally on the issues addressed there.

2. Here are 10 key words and phrases from this session for you to continue to play with in writing or art as you reflect on the personal implications of this teaching on the Cosmic Christ:

- The Christ Mystery

- Jesus of Nazareth

- Franciscans

- Eucharist

- Mystic Paul

- Incarnation

- The Material Universe

- Unitive Consciousness

- Truth is One

- Everything Sacred

Because Richard Rohr introduces us to an alternative to traditional orthodoxy, we close each session with a prayer that gives expression to orthodoxy while also allowing room for a contemporary theology.

We turn in this session to one of the leaders of the Protestant Reformation—Charles Wesley—who in 1740 gave expression to the mystic Christ in the words of this hymn which you can now say as a prayer, unless, of course you have a musician at hand who can lead you in the singing of it:

> Christ whose glory fills the skies,
> Christ the true, the only light,
> sun of righteousness arise,
> triumph o'er the shades of night.
> Dayspring from on high, be near;
> daystar, in my heart appear.
>
> Dark and cheerless is the morn
> unaccompanied by thee;
> Joyless is the day's return,
> till thy mercy's beams I see,
> till they inward light impart,
> glad my eyes and warm my heart.
>
> Visit then this soul of mine,
> pierce the gloom of sin and grief;
> fill me, radiancy divine,
> scatter all my unbelief;
> more and more thyself display,
> shining to the perfect day.

SESSION | 4

ORTHODOXY VS. ORTHOPRAXY

BEFORE THE SESSION

Many participants like to come to the group conversation after considering individually some of the issues that will be raised. The following five reflective activities are intended to open your mind, memories and emotions regarding some aspects of this session's topic. Use the space provided here to note your reflections.

1. This session is all about a return to Jesus' emphasis on lively practice following 2,000 years of Christian over-emphasis on right belief. The first option, Living Yourself Into a New Way of Thinking (p. 68), presents 15 quotes from Fr. Rohr drawn from the DVD. Read and reflect on those quotes as a way of anticipating the challenges of this session.

2. In this study, Richard Rohr refers repeatedly to the inspiring life of St. Francis, the most popular saint of all time. In addition to what we have heard before, in this session Richard offers further perspective on this remarkable spiritual genius:
   - Up to the point where Francis founded this order of mendicants, orders had been made up of monks and hermits who were more reclusive. The mendicants lived among the people and begged for their food.
   - In establishing a mendicant order, Francis was taking Jesus' directions to his disciples seriously: eat what is set before you; go into a house and receive the hospitality that is offered to you there. He was fundamentalist; but he was fundamentalist about the right things!
   - Francis's entire emphasis was on how you live. You live simply so that you might understand the crucified Christ. You live in solidarity with the crucified people so that you might know the pain of the world.
   - The reason Francis wasn't kicked out of the church was because he emphasized orthopraxy, not orthodoxy.
   - We are told that Francis would spend whole nights in caves or walking the roads of Italy saying over and over again, "Who am I?" and "Who are You?" The second "who" was the God he was seeking.

Take time to reflect on the life of Francis, perhaps drawing on other resources—books, films, Internet, local experts—as a way of extending your knowledge of this Christian spiritual leader who is second only to Jesus in his development of a practice in the Christian Way.

3. About Buddhism, Richard Rohr observes:

> *The reason so many people are attracted to Buddhism today is simply because for many hundreds of years they have meticulously observed the see-er: What happens when you do this? What happens when you think that? So they became masters of process which we now call practice.*

What is it that you have come to appreciate about Buddhism and other faiths that is a gift for you in your own journey of belief and practice?

4. Draw a timeline of your own life, noting the way that belief and practice have been woven into your journey with varying degrees of emphasis. Who have been the major influences in drawing your attention and your commitment to the centrality of orthopraxy (faithful practice) in our tradition?

5. In the second option, Soup Bowl Mutuality (p. 70), you will find a suggestion for group Bible discussion based on James 2:14-18. Read it now in anticipation of that conversation and see what word it has for you in your life at this time.

Sometimes in small group life you see some of the issues that Richard Rohr addresses in this session getting focused in the way that people treat one another. For example, there can be a risk of insistence on orthodoxy (right belief) undermining the gospel call to be fully present to one another with love and compassion. On the other hand, dominating and even charismatic individuals can insist on group practice that is not grounded in good theology.

The emphasis in this session on right practice comes to life in the way that the members of your group live their life together in these sessions. What practices have been established or have emerged which contribute to your group being a community of respect, nonjudgment, mutual sharing and compassion?

Before selecting from the following options, *watch the entire portion of the DVD for Session 4.*

OPTION 1: LIVING YOURSELF INTO
A NEW WAY OF THINKING

As you watch the DVD, you hear some memorable statements from Richard as he speaks about the priority of orthopraxy over orthodoxy. Here are 15 of those statements:

1. *You do not think yourself into a new way of living; you live yourself into a new way of thinking.*

2. *Every time the church split we lost half the gospel. The half we lost in 1054 at the Great Schism was contemplative practice.*

3. *Let the institutional church maintain the superstructure of creed, ritual and doctrine; that frees us to worry about the structure of our daily lives.*

4. *You can be perfectly orthodox and not understand the lifestyle of Jesus one bit!*

5. *Begging keeps you at the social level of everybody else, in their lives and in solidarity with their pain.*

6. *The great thing about orthopraxy is that there is really nothing to argue about until you do it! You don't believe something until you have done it.*

7. *We got lost in proving our metaphysics and then making others believe it. We spent all our time in enforcement, as if Jesus came to earth to enforce ideas.*

8. *I don't know a single example of any of our churches burning anyone at the stake for not taking care of the widows and orphans.*

9. *We live in a wonderful time when we see that faith is not about belonging systems or belief systems. If Christianity is going to be renewed and reformed, it has to move to practice-based Christianity.*

10. *The globalization of spirituality is making practice essential, because people don't believe you any more until you've done it. Most of the things we said we believed were no skin off our back!*

11. *The wonderful thing about orthopraxy is that it asks something of you. That's why we've avoided it for so long!*

12. *Going to a place in my daily prayers where for 20 minutes I have to go into this kenosis—this dying to myself, dying to my feelings, dying to my own angry thoughts—no one wants to do that!*

13. *Orthopraxy asks something of you. Orthodoxy allows you to be a policeman of other people and never really do it yourself. This gives you a false high moral ground without deserving it for a moment!*

14. *The word* orthodoxy *is not found in the scriptures. Jesus never encouraged this mentality, in fact, quite the contrary.*

15. *Isn't it ironic that a religion that believes that the word became flesh puts so much credence into words!*

1. Imagine a line down the center of your meeting space. This is a continuum. At one end is extreme orthodoxy (#1) and at the other extreme orthopraxy (#10). Of course there are many points on the continuum between the two extremes (#2-9). Choose a point that represents where you see the measure of your faith life in terms of these two ends of the continuum and go stand there.

2. While standing at your chosen spots on the continuum, go down the line from 1 to 10 and take turns explaining why you chose the points you chose.

3. After you've done that, everyone moves to a number that they would like to be at in future. Talk with someone near you about what you might do to realize that goal.

OPTION 2: SOUP BOWL MUTUALITY

Suzanne shares her concern about churches that serve food to the poor and homeless but only on condition that they hear a sermon. She advocates for a principle that says, "In order to get a bed and a bowl of soup you don't have to join my club."

In response, Richard offers insight about true mutuality of relationship:

- *The need to have people join your group to convince you that you are right is much more love of self than love of God.*
- *Christianity has largely been a belonging system instead of a transformational system. We have this attitude in our history that the best thing we can do for "them" is to present the gospel and get them to come to church.*
- *The assumption is that I've got the truth and you don't. I ensconce myself in a superior position.*
- *The great thing that our Catholic missionaries learned after they were in the mission for as little as three years can be summed up in this way: "I came to convert them and they converted me." Until that realization comes, the I-thou relationship of the true body of Christ hasn't happened.*
- *When the other has as much to teach me even though I'm the one providing the bowl of soup, that's mutuality.*
- *When I know what that other person has suffered and can hear their story and allow that story to influence me, that is the body of Christ re-formed.*

- *We can't maintain this one-sided evangelism where one group ensconces itself as the giver and keeps the other group co-dependent on them as the receiver and call that being like Jesus. I'm sure many people do that with the best of intentions, but very often it preserves them in a kind of hidden egocentricity.*

1. When have you had an experience anything like that of a missionary in which you were the one converted (transformed) in a situation where you thought that you were the converter?

2. It's quite possible that you have not risked the kind of vulnerability and transformation implied in this conversation. What yearning for personal change and growth emerges in you as you listen to Richard speaking about the challenges of the Way of Jesus and the promise therein?

3. Perhaps your church is involved in service to the poor, to the homeless, to people in extreme economic distress. What practices are in place that ensure that the system isn't one of co-dependence, conversion, superiority and egocentricity?

4. Richard makes reference to a passage from the letter of James, James 2:14-18. Read it together and see what meaning it has for you as you struggle with this matter of a life as envisioned by Jesus and the early Christian community.

OPTION 3: GOOD THEOLOGY STILL MATTERS

The emphasis in this session on orthopraxy leads Doug to raise the critical matter of concepts and belief:

> We are incapable of having a content-less mind. So what difference does it make what we believe conceptually?

In affirming that good theology is important, Richard raises a historical situation in New Mexico that involved the Franciscans:

> When they were withdrawn for political reasons, the Franciscans trained laymen to run the church with no priests. For more than 100 years these sincere, well-intentioned laymen ran the church without any infusion of good theology. In that time the church became very guilt-centered, punitive and moralistic. That's an extreme example of how devolved Christianity can get if you have no content with good sources. What happens is you get charismatic, manipulative and dominant personalities taking over. It's true in any institution: the loudest and most manipulative personality controls the show. So you finally have a choice between good teaching and good thinking, or a cult of personality. I can talk this way because the Franciscans gave me excellent education in theology. You get to know the "big Tradition," then you can critique the "small tradition."

1. How do you ensure that your practice is grounded in good theology?

2. When have you been aware of situations where practice was grounded in bad theology?

OPTION 4: WAITING FOR THE GOD EXPERIENCE

Richard offers some observations on why it is that most people who have no experience of Holy Presence are unable to sustain a contemplative practice:

The Center has been here 27 years now. I've seen the vast majority of people experiment with contemplation but not last. If you haven't had a previous experience of an actual lover/presence/encounter/person you don't know what you're waiting for. You get tired of waiting for an energy or idea or "enlightenment." If they haven't had a Jesus encounter of any type—a baptism in the Spirit, as charismatics would call it—I find that by and large most people give up on contemplation.

I find again and again in my own experience here that people who stay with it are people who already know that there's someone to wait for, that God is real. They're not trying to manufacture God experience; they're trying to deepen already existing God experience. It really gives me sympathy and patience for people who give up. They don't know what they're waiting for or if it's worth waiting for. Contemplative prayer doesn't give you a lot of pay-off if you're not committed to the practice itself.

1. How are people in your discussion group being sustained in their contemplative practice through a real experience of Presence or encounter with the Divine?

2. And what about the absence of that experience? How have you been sustained in your desire for a deepening relationship with God even when there is no word? (*The word of God was rare in those days; visions were not widespread.* 1 Samuel 3:1)

OPTION 5: FALLING UPWARD

Doug says:

> *I'd like to hear you, Richard, talking more about keeping people engaged in pursuing that experience even if they haven't had it.*

Richard responds:

> *The reason I wrote* Falling Upward *is because I feel for the vast majority the falling experience, which is inevitable if you are living a real human life, is the normal path of transformation. I say in* Naked Now *that great love and great suffering are the classic paths. You don't fall into great love or great suffering without falling. You don't go there intentionally. It's always outside your control: I can't succeed at this; I don't look good; I just lost my house…my money…my marriage. We don't want to wish these things on anybody but, again and again, you see these are the things that catapult people into the second stage of life, or unitive experience. We know we can't program those, but we clergy were given the impression that's what Sunday was about. We would program a religious experience.*

1. What do you understand to be the significance of the title of Richard's book, *Falling Upward?*

2. In what ways have you experienced this great truth of human life—that the falling experience is the normal path of transformation?

OPTION 6: ACCOMPANIMENT

The conversation brings the group around to a consideration of the importance of accompaniment:

> There's a task we have to accompany people so that they can give language to their experience in a way that leads them beyond the practice to deeper consciousness. We often don't have the words.

Richard states:

> We only have the language of faith as assent to doctrine. That's totally inadequate to the inner experience. The ministry of spiritual direction (accompaniment) is growing broadly. There is a recognition of it in Buddhism and Judaism as well. In the matter of accompaniment, there have to be elders who are at least one step beyond you. I want someone to be a little ahead of me. Those kind of people as teachers and learners are just proliferating today. It's wonderful.

Who is it who accompanies you in enabling you to put into words and awareness your experience of the divine? What access do you have to someone who is trained as a spiritual director?

OPTION 7: PERSONAL REFLECTION

(for use following the session)

The emphasis of this session has been so much on practice that there must have been many points in the process where you were aware of your way of being in the world being addressed. In your reflection time after the session, take these moments of personal insight and continue to look at them as opportunities for supporting your growth in faith.

CLOSING

Because Richard Rohr introduces us to an alternative to traditional orthodoxy, we close each session with a prayer that gives expression to orthodoxy while also allowing room for a contemporary theology.

Psalm 107 is one of several psalms sung by pilgrims coming to Jerusalem to celebrate one of the Jewish festivals, giving thanks for having been brought safely through dangers of many kinds.

This contemporary poetic rendering by Nan Merrill brings this ancient writing into the foreground of our concern for orthopraxy that connects us to the Divine mystery in all things.

One: Who will offer the dance of their own life as a creation of devotion and beauty?

Many: Only those who have come through the darkness and walk now in the Light can offer their lives in service to build the new world, where justice and freedom will truly flourish.

One: Awaken, all you who are yet asleep, let us plant seeds for the commingling of heaven and earth;

Many: For the Energy of love radiates in everything, and receptive hearts are purified by its Fire.

One: Blessed are the children of Light, for they know their home in the Universal Heart.

Many: Let your heart be clear and simple, and your soul filled with Light;

One: Enter the place of gentleness, the heart-space of the Beloved, the embodiment of Love!

Many: For we are invited to radiate the Divine Presence, to be blessing to one another;

One: Thus do we become the very image that we reflect.

Many: Whoever is wise, let them ponder these things, let all people reflect on the gifts of the Beloved.

—Psalm 107:33-43 in *Psalms for Praying: An Invitation to Wholeness*
by Nan C. Merrill (Harrisburg, PA: Continuum, 1996, pp. 230-231)

NAME

Kim	Romeo	Tony
30	75	30
42	70 ✕	🗲🗲
3	36+	11
49	7	47

SESSION | 5

MYSTICISM OVER MORALISM

BEFORE THE SESSION

Many participants like to come to the group conversation after considering individually some of the issues that will be raised. The following five reflective activities are intended to open your mind, memories and emotions regarding some aspects of this session's topic. Use the space provided here to note your reflections.

1. In Option 2, The Weaker I Get; The Stronger I Become (p. 80), three passages from three of Paul's letters are presented for reflection within the theme of that section. Take time to read and sit with these passages, allowing the word that is there for you to emerge and touch you.

2. In the DVD presentation, you will hear Fr. Rohr speak of the need to help people understand that they *have* had experiences of God. As he says, "Most people have 'God experiences,' but there's no one to tell them, 'You just had it! That moment of communion you had with your little baby while you were breast-feeding today—that's it! That moment of enjoying that wildflower and feeling that jerk of joy in your heart—that's it!'" This week, notice when you have God experiences. Have you ever been aware of times when someone else has helped you to see that you did indeed have a graced moment? When have you accompanied someone else in their recognition of God's presence in the ordinariness of their life?

3. In Option 4, No More Counting (p. 84), you will find a poetic reflection by Richard Rohr as he offers a final word on what it means to truly arrive in the second half of life where the soul takes over from the ego and you more easily break from the American culture of entitlement. Use that reflection as a catalyst for reflection, perhaps for your own writing prior to the session. You might use one of these lines as a beginning line for your own poetic reflection:
   - *Here in this second half of life…*
   - *The counting game is over.*
   - *But then there's the world of grace…*
   - *All you can do is give thanks, because it's totally undeserved.*
   - *The Grace of God [frees] us from the burden of counting.*

4. As you come to the final session in the series of five, take time to think about the other members of the group—what they have contributed to your learning, what they have chosen to reveal of themselves, what has opened for them as a result of the teaching of Richard Rohr. Hold each one of them with love and respect, opening your heart and letting go of whatever would keep you from closing well with each one of them.

5. Take time to go back over all that you have done in these five sessions, appreciating the totality of Richard's teaching on *Alternative Orthodoxy, The Legacy of St. Francis.*

In this final session make sure to leave time for these aspects of group closure:
- wrapping up whatever is unfinished
- expressing appreciation for the contributions made by each member
- hearing the difference it has made for each person to participate (see Option 5: A Graced Closure, p. 86)
- giving thanks to God for the gifts, insights, relationships and sacred guidance of this time
- cleaning up the meeting space

You have been on a journey over these five sessions, a journey that has either *introduced* you to the worldview and theology of Fr. Richard Rohr or *taken you further* into his perspective on an alternative orthodoxy rooted in the Franciscan tradition.

In this final session:

- You will focus on a new aspect of Richard's teaching: Mysticism over Moralism.
- You will come to the end of a five-session process that has introduced you to an alternative orthodoxy, a gift within the legacy of St. Francis.
- You will encounter again dominant themes that were introduced in the previous four sessions.
- You will come to a closing with the other people who have been part of this learning process with you.
- You will pause to how this learning experience has deepened your understanding of God and faith.

 Before selecting from the following options, *watch the entire portion of the DVD for Session 5.*

OPTION 1: MORALISM, MYSTICISM AND YOU

As you've seen and heard, Richard Rohr names things as he sees them! In one moment he uncovers religious dysfunction and holds it up to the light; in the next he presents a vision of relationship with God that is transformative and inspiring. Given the breadth of the territory, it's inevitable that Richard touches themes in your own journey of religious and spiritual growth.

From the 10 statements below, choose one or two that connect with your own story in some way. Share, either with one or two other people or with the members of your small group, how these statements in some way speak to your own experience or the experience of people close to you:

1. People who are initially attracted to religion are people who like social order. They think that God came to earth to be a policeman. This attention to social order in religion has a place in the first half of life when the ego needs to be contained in boundaries. If you stay in this first half of life religion, you stay at the moralistic level.

2. Scripture, Jesus, the mystics and saints recognized that the goal of religion is not a perfect moral stance, but union with God.

3. Union with God is achieved by doing things wrong rather than by doing things right. Perfection is not the goal.

4. Moralism is less concerned with love and more concerned with creating an ego identity that can hold the moral high ground. Too often the heads of religion are involved in finding sinners and in managing sin.

5. We see Jesus exposing ugly morality throughout the gospels. It's always the same story: the one who is always wrong is, in Jesus' eyes, revealed as right.

6. What undoes moralism is a moment of unitive consciousness, a moment of grace, a moment of unearned love, a moment of forgiveness, a moment of unmerited consolation. That's the only thing that breaks down the *quid pro quo* world of morality.

7. God has come to save us all by grace. The mystics have no trouble surrendering to that. For Bonaventure, God is a fountain full of outflowing love, only flowing in one direction, always and forever. There is no wrath in God; there is no anger in God. There is only outpouring love.

8. You will obsess about moralism if you don't get to the mystical level. You become more anal-retentive the older you get when you haven't experienced God. It's not joyful; it's not a wedding banquet; it's not happiness. You get more desperate, more impatient, and you want more laws to obey.

9. When you get moralistic, it's not long before you get violent. When you are sure you are on higher moral ground than other people, it's very quick that you have a right to torture them, exclude them, punish them, kill them and, as Jesus says in John's Gospel, when you do it you will think you are doing a holy duty for God.

10. The mind that emerges from mystical experience, from second-half-of-life maturity is the contemplative mind. You don't calculate life; you contemplate life. If you want to grease the wheels to second-half-of-life consciousness—to the mystical level—the best way is to contemplate.

OPTION 2: THE WEAKER I GET, THE STRONGER I BECOME!

Richard spoke enthusiastically about Paul in Session 3 and returns again with glowing affirmation of Paul's understanding of the mystery of the cross. Here are some key lines to remind you of what Richard said about Paul:

- *If you take the whole corpus of Paul, it's 90% mystical.*
- *Paul reveals that all these constructs to create order in the world are doomed to failure.*
- *Paul's key for creating* order *in the universe is by introducing* disorder *at its center. That's what he means by the mystery of the cross.*
- *Your only ordered world is your ability to deal with disorder and failure.*
- *Paul introduced a new order that is recognizing, honoring and using disorder for good purpose.*

Below are three passages from three of Paul's letters. Read each of these aloud and discuss:

- Where in his writing do you see Paul giving expression to the interplay between moralism and mysticism that Richard is uncovering in this session? Feel free to go to other passages from his letters that come to mind.
- Paul may not have anticipated that his letters would be read not only by the folks in Corinth, Rome and Galatia, but also by us. What would you say to Paul in response to the passion and vulnerability of his writing?

Galatians 2:19-21 (The Message)

What actually took place is this: I tried keeping rules and working my head off to please God, and it didn't work. So I quit being a "law man" so that I could be *God's* man. Christ's life showed me how, and enabled me to do it. I identified myself completely with him. Indeed, I have been crucified with Christ. My ego is no longer central. It is no longer important that I appear righteous before you or have your good opinion, and I am no longer driven to impress God. Christ lives in me. The life you see me living is not "mine," but it is lived by faith in the Son of God, who loved me and gave himself for me. I am not going to go back on that.

Is it not clear to you that to go back to that old rule-keeping, peer-pleasing religion would be an abandonment of everything personal and free in my relationship with God? I refuse to do that, to repudiate God's grace. If a living relationship with God could come by rule-keeping, then Christ died unnecessarily.

Romans 7:4-6 (NRSV)

In the same way, my friends, you have died to the law through the body of Christ, so that you may belong to another, to him who has been raised from the dead in order that we may bear fruit for God. While we were living in the flesh, our sinful passions, aroused by the law, were at work in our members to bear fruit for death. But now we are discharged from the law, dead to that which held us captive, so that we are slaves not under the old written code but in the new life of the Spirit.

2 Corinthians 12:7-10 (The Message)

Because of the extravagance of those revelations, and so I wouldn't get a big head, I was given the gift of a handicap to keep me in constant touch with my limitations. Satan's angel did his best to get me down; what he in fact did was push me to my knees. No danger then of walking around high and mighty! At first I didn't think of it as a gift, and begged God to remove it. Three times I did that, and then he told me,

> My grace is enough; it's all you
> need.
> My strength comes into its own
> in your weakness.

Once I heard that, I was glad to let it happen. I quit focusing on the handicap and began appreciating the gift. It was a case of Christ's strength moving in on my weakness. Now I take limitations in stride, and with good cheer, these limitations that cut me down to size—abuse, accidents, opposition, bad breaks. I just let Christ take over! And so the weaker I get, the stronger I become.

OPTION 3: GROWING MYSTICS

Doug opens up an exploration of how churches can both be a barrier to the experience of God as well as a community to open up that experience when he asks:

> Essentially, you're saying that the destiny of every Christian is to be a mystic. That seems so implausible that we put it off to the next life! I say to folks (half joking) that I set out to be a mystic and then got ordained. The sheer busyness of the job rendered it nearly impossible. I can see individuals and small groups coming together to enter into that kind of unitive consciousness and I can see that having an effect in action, but how in the world do you make it a bigger phenomenon?

Richard responds:

> When I say mystical, I mean experiential. It is possible if we get out of the realm of law and doctrine. Most people have God experiences but there's no one to tell them, "You just had it!" We've made it a churchy thing as we ministers well know: you've had it when you've been around candlesticks and vestments. This is why we get back to this need for spiritual direction—wise people who can say, "That moment of communion you had with your little baby while you were breast feeding today—that's it! That moment of enjoying that wildflower and feeling that jerk of joy in your heart—that's it!" We need to un-churchify the gospel. It's just too darn churchified! People are having religious experiences and don't know it.

In the conversation that follows Richard's reflection, the members of the group open up various aspects of this matter of church as a block to mystical experience or church as a guide in that process. Allow their conversation to be a source of reflection for yours:

1. Raymond asks:

> Can church be a place where people are helped to identify the presence of God in their everyday lives, a place where people can talk together about how their everyday lives are an experience of God?

What would it take for church to be more like that? What success have you had in creating that kind of opportunity?

2. Suzanne asserts that people can have experiences of God in any moment quite apart from the presence of a priest, rabbi or preacher. The other members of the group support that, and Richard speaks about "the training into subtle consciousness" that is required as individuals move to this deepening practice of Presence. The group recognize the power of community in this process, and Richard underscores the need for communal support of the individual:

> If there isn't community holding you accountable to what you say you've experienced, helping you unpack your experience, it doesn't go anywhere. I could be heard to be encouraging individualism, but I'm not. That doesn't go anywhere. We're social beings. Unless I let your holiness rub off on me, I won't experience my own. As Jesus said, "Where two or three are gathered in my name, there I am." We have a total promise of presence, just as strong as in the bread and the wine.

Talk together about the power of community (whatever size) to be a place for holding you accountable in the growth of your mystical consciousness, as well as a setting in which you become ever clearer about the daily presence of God in your life.

OPTION 4: NO MORE COUNTING

Richard offers this final reflection at the end of the five sessions:

>Here in this second half of life—
>>the mystical, the contemplative, the adult Christian—
>
>you stop counting and let God stop counting.
>
>The counting game is over.
>The ego counts; the soul experiences.
>It lets it be and learns from it, but it doesn't weigh and measure.
>
>Here in this American culture of entitlement—
>>people counting what they deserve
>>>and think they have a right to—
>
>entitlement creates unlikable people.
>We worry about our children growing up
>>in an entirely entitled society.
>
>But then there's the world of grace—
>>the world of the gospel,
>>the world of mercy.
>
>It's all gratitude and confidence,
>>the confidence
>>given by God's gratuitous choice and love
>
>to use you as an instrument,
>to dwell in you.
>
>Validated at the deepest inner level:
>>no need to be rich,
>>no need to be famous,
>>no need to be good-looking,
>>no need to think that I'm better than you.
>
>The need itself is taken away.
>
>If you can just notice in your own mind and emotions
>>whenever you're counting
>>or thinking God is counting,
>
>that's not where you want to be.
>It's a waste of time.
>It's finally self-defeating.
>Organized religion creates membership requirements,
>>and then you're right back into counting.

The gospel
        is a great leveling
        of the playing field.
All of us equally carry that divine image.
All you can do is give thanks, because it's totally undeserved.
It has nothing to do with you:
        gift, gift, gift, gift, gift.

The grace of God freeing us
        from the burden of counting.

1. What insights and practices will you take away from this series that will help you give up counting?

2. How will you support yourself in being *in* the culture of entitlement without being *of* that culture?

OPTION 5: A GRACED CLOSURE

When the group that met with Richard in Albuquerque came to their closing time, they each identified gifts of insight and commitment that they were taking from their time together:

Suzanne, following the stimulation of Richard's teaching and the group conversation, will pursue further reading and exploration of this kind, but without losing the simplicity of the life that Jesus and St. Francis present to us.

Doug, recognizing that small groups are much more his faith community than the institutional church, will continue to gather communities of "credulous listeners," where people can acknowledge the experiences of God that they all have and all desire.

Joe, in receiving permission to abandon "the scorecard," intends to get down to more simple processes of relating to God in the company of a community that will support him on that journey.

Jennifer takes from this time a deep appreciation for this alternative orthodoxy, through which she now sees that God *always* planned to meet us in the flesh, not because we were bad, but because God wanted to be with us.

Raymond goes with a powerful sense of mysticism, not as something remote and out there some place, but as something as intimate as every breath we take. He goes with awareness that every breath he takes is a contact with God. God happens.

What are *you* each taking from this time of learning in community?

OPTION 6: PERSONAL REFLECTION

(for use following the session)

1. Make time to complete any of the Options that you didn't have time for during the session.

2. As you conclude this final session in the series of five, recall what you've learned from the other members of the group, what they chose to reveal of themselves, and what opened for each of them as a result of Richard's teaching. Hold members with gratitude, love and respect in a time of prayer and meditation.

3. Take time to go back over all that you did in these five sessions, appreciating the totality of Richard's teaching on *Embracing an Alternative Orthodoxy: The Legacy of St. Francis.*

OPTION 7: CLOSING

Because Richard Rohr introduced us to an alternative to traditional orthodoxy, we closed our sessions with prayers that gave expression to orthodoxy while also allowing room for a contemporary theology.

We close this session and this five-part study with the words of an 8th-century Irish hymn that is still found in many hymnals, "Be Thou My Vision" (found on the next page).

If you don't have musical leaders at hand, you can find creative ways to read the words together (for example, responsively or in unison). As you say or sing the words, wonder if this old Irish hymn ever made it across the waterways and pathways of Europe to Assisi, where Francis and his community walked in humble service to their neighbors.

BE THOU MY VISION

Be thou my vision, O joy of my heart;
naught be all else to me save that thou art,
thou my best thought, by day or by night,
waking or sleeping thy presence my light.

Be thou my wisdom, my calm in all strife;
I ever with thee, and thou in my life;
thou loving parent, thy child may I be,
thou in me dwelling and I one with thee.

Riches I heed not, nor vain empty praise,
thou mine inheritance, now and always;
thou and thou only, the first in my heart,
great God of heaven, my treasure thou art.

Great God of heaven, after victory won,
may I reach heaven's joys, O bright heaven's sun!
Heart of my own heart, whatever befall,
Still be my vision, O ruler of all.

Irish ca. 8th century; translated by Mary Elizabeth Byrne, 1905;
version by Eleanor H. Hull, 1912.

SUGGESTED RESOURCES

Center for Action and Contemplation

Home of THE ROHR INSTITUTE
An Educational Center Grounded in the Christian Mystical Tradition

If you like what you have experienced in this introduction to an alternative orthodoxy and the teaching of Richard Rohr, here are resources to enable you to continue your journey of learning with Richard and the folks at the Rohr Institute:

- Go to the website of CAC—www.cac.org—to learn about programs, resources and other learning opportunities of the Center and The Rohr Institute.
- At the website be sure to sign up for *Richard Rohr's Daily Meditations* which will come to you free by email every day.
- Subscribe to the new journal of alternative orthodoxy, *ONEING*, as a way to stay connected to emergent writing by many great authors.
- Continue to explore some of the life-shaping themes opened by Richard in this series, by reading his book, *Falling Upward: A Spirituality for the Two Halves of Life*.
- Connect to the Webcasts of the Rohr Institute and engage in learning processes animated by Richard Rohr and enriched by other learners from around the world.
- Choose from other books by Richard Rohr, discerning the focus of your learning from many titles:
  — *Immortal Diamond: The Search for Our True Self*
  — *The Naked Now: Learning to See as the Mystics See*
  — *Everything Belongs: The Gift of Contemplative Prayer*
  — *Things Hidden: Scripture as Spirituality*
  — *Soul Brothers: Men in the Bible Speak to Men Today*
  — *Simplicity: The Art of Living*

NOTES

NOTES

NOTES

NOTES

NOTES

NOTES